Please renew or return items by the date
shown on your receipt

www.hertfordshire.gov.uk/libraries

Renewals and enquiries: 0300 123 4049

Textphone for hearing or 0300 123 4041
speech impaired users:

L32 11.16

Hertfordshire

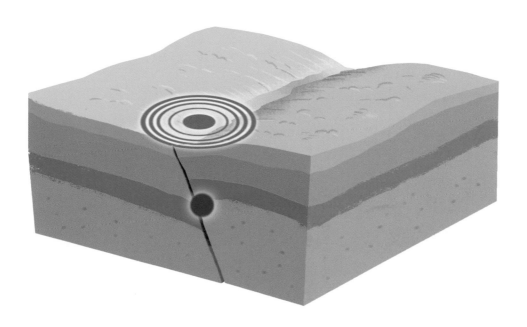

Author:
Alex Woolf studied history at Essex University, England. He is the author of over 60 books for children, including *The Science of Rocks and Minerals: The Hard Truth About the Stuff Beneath Our Feet, You Wouldn't Want to Live Without Poo!* and *You Wouldn't Want to Live Without Vegetables!*

Artists:
Andy Rowland
Bryan Beach

Editor:
Jacqueline Ford

Published in Great Britain in MMXVIII by Book House, an imprint of
The Salariya Book Company Ltd
25 Marlborough Place, Brighton BN1 1UB
www.salariya.com

HB ISBN: 978-1-912233-24-3
PB ISBN: 978-1-912233-75-5

1 3 5 7 9 8 6 4 2

A CIP catalogue record for this book is available from the British Library.

Printed and bound in China.

Visit
www.salariya.com
for our online catalogue and
free fun stuff.

PAPER FROM
SUSTAINABLE
FORESTS

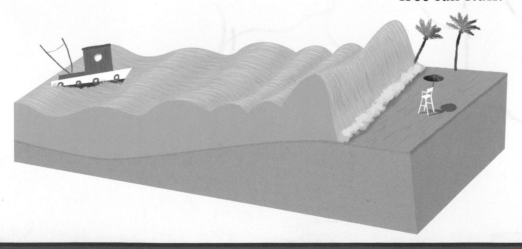

The Science of Natural Disasters

The Devastating Truth About Volcanoes, Earthquakes and Tsunamis

Written by
Alex Woolf

Illustrated by
Andy Rowland

BOOK HOUSE
a SALARIYA imprint

Contents

Introduction

The Earth provides for all our needs. It gives us air to breathe, food to eat and fresh water to drink. But our planet can also be violent and destructive. Volcanoes erupt, sending out clouds of ash and rivers of molten lava. Earthquakes shake up the land, destroying buildings and sparking destructive fires. Tsunamis – enormous ocean waves – crash onto the shore, devastating coastal communities.

In this book we'll look at how and where volcanoes, earthquakes and tsunamis happen, and their powerful impact on people and the environment. And we'll investigate how, with better scientific understanding of these disasters, we may be able to reduce tragic losses of life in the future.

Cracks in the crust

Currents within the mantle set the tectonic plates drifting across the globe. They move very slowly, at around 2.5 to 15 cm (1 to 6 in) per year, but they never stop.

Convergent faults

At a convergent fault, tectonic plates push into each other. As a result of these collisions, earthquakes and volcanoes are common in these areas. In some cases, mountain ranges form.

The mountain's rising faster than you are.

The hard, rocky surface of Earth is called the crust. Beneath the crust is the mantle, a layer of semi-molten rock thousands of miles deep. The crust isn't one solid layer. It is broken up into about thirty sections called tectonic plates. These plates fit together like a giant jigsaw puzzle to cover the whole surface of the Earth. The boundaries where the tectonic plates meet are called faults. It is along these faults that most earthquakes and volcanic eruptions happen. When an earthquake or volcanic eruption occurs under or near the ocean, it can trigger a tsunami. There are three kinds of faults: convergent, divergent and transform.

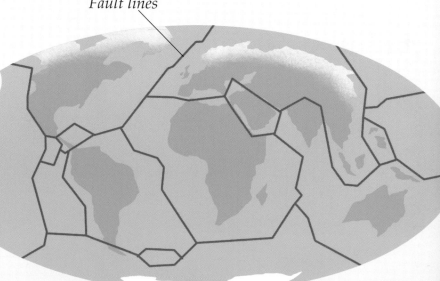

Fault lines

Divergent faults

At divergent faults, plates move apart, causing volcanic activity as magma (molten rock) from the mantle rises to fill the gap. The magma cools to form new land. This process is happening right now, beneath the Atlantic Ocean. As a result, the Atlantic is growing by a few inches each year.

I swear it takes longer to cross the Atlantic each time!

Transform faults

At transform faults, plates grind against each other as they move in opposite directions. Transform faults can lead to earthquakes. Most, but not all, are on the ocean floor. There is one in California, USA, called the San Andreas Fault, where one plate is moving south and the other north. As a result, California suffers regular earthquakes.

It was San Andreas's Fault.

Around 250 million years ago, the Earth had just one vast landmass called Pangaea. Gradually, over millions of years, the movement of the tectonic plates caused Pangaea to break up, creating the world as it is today.

Fascinating fact

Iceland is on the Mid-Atlantic Ridge, the divergent fault in the middle of the Atlantic Ocean. As a result, there are cracks in the landscape where rock has been torn apart. Iceland also experiences a lot of volcanic activity, leading to the formation of new rock and new islands.

There's a great belt of volcanoes around the edge of the Pacific Ocean, known as the Ring of Fire.

How volcanoes form

Volcanoes form in places where magma forces its way out of a crack in the Earth's crust. This can happen at divergent faults, where two tectonic plates move apart, allowing magma to rise to the surface. Most of these volcanoes are located on the seafloor. Volcanoes can also occur at convergent faults, where two plates collide. One plate slides under the other and moves down into the mantle. This is called subduction, and the area where it happens is the subduction zone. The lower plate partially melts in the mantle, making new magma that rises up to form volcanoes.

Hot spots

Some volcanoes form in the middle of tectonic plates, far from the boundaries, in hot spots. These are places where the hot mantle melts, forces its way through the crust, and erupts as lava. Hot-spot volcanoes in the oceans form underwater mountains called seamounts. The Hawaiian Islands are the summits of giant seamounts.

Oahu   Maui   Hawaii

Hawaiian islands   Hot spot

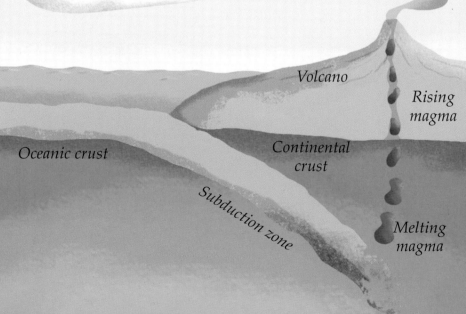

Volcano

Oceanic crust

Continental crust

Subduction zone

Rising magma

Melting magma

Parts of a volcano

Most volcanoes are shaped like cones. The cone is made up of layers of solidified lava and ash from past eruptions. Beneath the volcano is a magma chamber. Magma rises through a central tube called a vent, erupting from the crater at the top. Magma may also erupt from side vents.

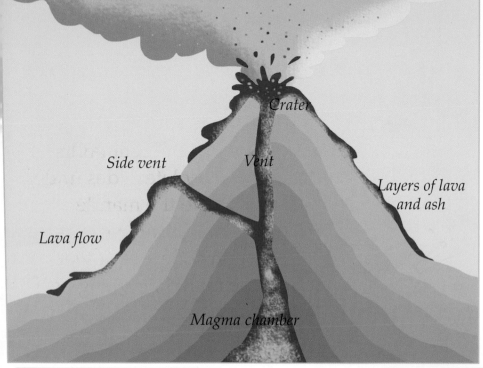

Crater

Side vent

Vent

Layers of lava and ash

Lava flow

Magma chamber

Active, dormant and extinct

I can't tell if he's dormant or extinct.

Active volcanoes are volcanoes that have erupted in the past 10,000 years. Dormant volcanoes are volcanoes that have not erupted in the past 10,000 years, but experts think they are still capable of erupting. Extinct volcanoes are volcanoes that nobody expects will erupt again.

Lava varies depending on the kind of rock it's formed from. Some types flow easily like syrup; other types are thick and sticky like tar.

Fascinating fact

The word *volcano* comes from Vulcan, the Roman god of fire. According to legend, Vulcan lived on the island of Vulcano off the south-west coast of Italy. He worked as a blacksmith making weapons for the other gods. The Romans believed the eruptions from the island's volcano were sparks from Vulcan's forge.

Fountains and explosions

Stratovolcanoes

The magma at convergent faults, where stratovolcanoes form, is thick and sticky. It blocks the volcano's vent until the pressure from the magma chamber becomes too great, and the volcano erupts in a huge explosion.

Volcanic eruptions are not all the same. Some are gentle while others can be explosive. Each type of eruption builds different kinds of volcano. Gentle eruptions, which happen at divergent faults and hot spots, build shield volcanoes. These are wide and low with sloping sides, like an upside-down plate. Shield volcanoes erupt frequently. Explosive eruptions, which happen at convergent faults, build steep-sided, cone-shaped volcanoes called stratovolcanoes. These volcanoes erupt only rarely, and the eruptions are usually violent and dangerous.

In 1991 Mount Pinatubo, a stratovolcano in the Philippines, erupted. The explosion blew 300 metres (984 ft) off the top of the mountain and formed an eruption column 40 km (25 miles) high.

Go on then! Show us what you can do!

Don't tempt me!

Kilauea, a shield volcano in Hawaii, is the most active volcano on Earth. Erupting almost constantly since 1983, it produces lava fountains that shoot up to 0.8 km (half a mile) into the air.

Shield volcanoes

Shield volcanoes produce lava that is fluid and runny. Gas in the lava makes it shoot upwards like a fountain. After falling back to Earth, the lava flows down the volcano in glowing red rivers called lava flows. Two types of lava are produced: pahoehoe and aa. When it cools, pahoehoe has a smooth, ropy surface, while aa has a rough, lumpy surface.

No, pahoehoe.

Aaaah!

Pyroclastic flows

When eruption columns get too heavy, they collapse and sweep down the volcano's side in a pyroclastic flow. These red-hot avalanches can travel up to 160 km (100 miles) per hour, destroying everything in their path. In 79 AD, a pyroclastic flow from Mount Vesuvius engulfed the Roman town of Pompeii. The town was preserved under the ash and pumice.

Try it yourself

Do this experiment outside to avoid making a mess. Place a small jar in a mound of dirt. Add two spoonfuls of baking soda, a spoonful of dish soap and a few drops of red food colouring. Now for the eruption! Add 30 ml of vinegar. The vinegar and baking soda will react, causing a beautiful spout of 'lava'!

Baking soda

Dish soap

Food colouring

Jar

Vinegar

The impact of eruptions

When the volcano Nevado del Ruiz in Colombia erupted in 1985, it created a lahar. The lahar hit the town of Armero 50 km (30 miles) away, killing 21,000 residents.

Environmental effects

Pyroclastic flows scorch the ground, knocking down trees and killing animals. Eruption columns are blown thousands of kilometres around the Earth. They can deposit layers of ash that kill plants and turn green wilderness into grey desert.

Volcanic eruptions change the landscape. Volcanoes themselves begin as vents in the ground, which gradually build up into mountains of ash and lava. Undersea eruptions create seamounts that may eventually form volcanic islands. When lava cools and solidifies it makes new rock, called igneous rock. Violent eruptions can blow the tops off volcanoes and throw out tonnes of ash and rock that spread for many kilometres. The volcano's crater becomes an enormous 'caldera' – the biggest of which can be more than 50 km (30 miles) across.

Lahars

A lahar is a muddy mixture of water and volcanic ash that flows down the sides of a volcano and into surrounding valleys. Lahars can rush along at more than 145 kph (90 mph), carrying trees, boulders and other debris with them, and destroying towns and villages.

Why it happens

Lahars are made up of volcanic ash and water. The water comes from snow and ice from the volcano summit, from thunderstorms that form inside eruption columns and from rainfall after the eruption. The water and ash mix to form a thick, sticky mud that can travel for more than 160 km (100 miles). When it finally stops, the mud sets hard like concrete.

Human impacts

Half a billion people live in places at risk from volcanoes. Many choose to live there because volcanoes produce fertile soil for farming, volcanic rock makes an excellent building material and volcanoes provide heat for electricity. Yet when volcanic eruptions strike they can be devastating, burying farmland and damaging roads and power supplies.

In 2010, the volcano Ejafjallajökull in Iceland erupted, sending up 250 million cubic metres (9 billion cubic feet) of ash. Fears that it would damage aircraft engines led to the cancellation of thousands of flights.

13

How earthquakes happen

In 1906 a massive earthquake shook San Francisco, USA, overturning stoves and gas lamps and causing fires to engulf the city. The city burned for three days, and at least 3,000 people were killed.

Foreshocks and aftershocks

Before a big earthquake, there may be foreshocks – smaller tremors as the ground begins to shift. Tremors may also be felt after an earthquake as the plates settle into their new position. These are called aftershocks.

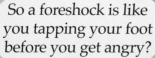

Almost all earthquakes happen at faults in Earth's crust (see pages 6–7), where tectonic plates push or grind against each other. This is not a smooth movement. The plate edges rub against each other, causing a build-up of tension. Finally, when the pressure becomes too great, the plates suddenly lurch into a new position. This abrupt movement sends vibrations through the ground, which we experience as an earthquake. The ground then settles, but over the years the tension builds up again, leading to another quake.

So a foreshock is like you tapping your foot before you get angry?

This is getting stressful – I have to move!

Okay, but it may shake things up a little.

Focus and epicentre

The place where the rocks first shatter and the earthquake begins is called the focus, and it's usually deep underground.

The point directly above this on the Earth's surface, where the damage is often the greatest, is the epicentre.

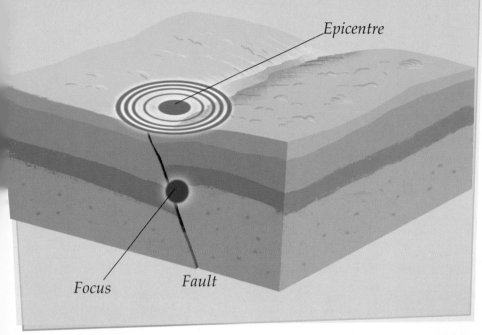

Epicentre

Focus

Fault

Seismic waves

Earthquakes release tremors called seismic waves. Some are body waves, travelling through the Earth. Others are surface waves. The two kinds of surface waves are Love waves and Rayleigh waves.

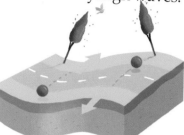

Love waves move side to side

Rayleigh waves move up and down

The first body waves (called primary waves) travel outwards from the focus at over 24,000 kph (15,000 mph). A second set of waves (secondary waves) follows after at a slower rate.

Can you believe it?

Animals tend to be more sensitive than humans to ground tremors. In 1975, the Chinese city of Haicheng was evacuated because the animals were acting strangely. Cows and horses were restless. Chickens refused to enter their coops. Several hours later, the city was destroyed by a massive earthquake.

He's showing us there's going to be an earthquake!

Or he's just showing off.

The Mercalli scale is used to measure the damage caused by an earthquake. The scale goes from I (detected only by scientific instruments) to XII (complete devastation – all structures destroyed).

Haiti earthquake

In 2010, a powerful earthquake struck the Caribbean nation of Haiti. It caused about 316,000 deaths and left 1.5 million people homeless. The earthquake was followed by around 52 powerful aftershocks.

Most earthquakes don't last very long – usually less than a minute. But the damage they cause can be long-lasting. Buildings crack and crumble. Roads, bridges and railways are twisted apart. Long after the shaking stops, damaged structures continue to collapse. People are rarely killed by the earthquake itself; they are crushed by falling buildings or else perish in fires that follow. If earthquakes strike in rural areas where there aren't many buildings, casualties are much lower.

Measuring earthquakes

Seismologists (earthquake experts) have developed scales to describe the strength of an earthquake. One is the Richter scale, which gives an earthquake a number to indicate how much ground movement it causes. Quakes below 3 cannot be felt by people. A very severe quake measures over 8.

I'd give him an 8.1 on the Richter scale.

In July 1976, an earthquake measuring 7.8 on the Richter scale struck Tangshan in China, destroying 85 percent of the city. It was one of the deadliest earthquakes in history.

More disasters

Earthquakes often trigger further disasters, which can sometimes be even more deadly than the original event. Damage to gas and electricity supplies can spark major fires.

If quakes have left the ground unstable, landslides, mudslides and avalanches can follow. In coastal regions, quake damage to sea walls often leads to floods.

Seismologists

How can seismologists calculate an earthquake's epicentre? They use highly sensitive instruments called seismographs to measure ground tremors. Seismographs in three separate locations can, together, pinpoint the epicentre.

In October 2005, a powerful quake hit Kashmir. Food, tents, clothing and medicine soon began arriving. But rescue efforts were delayed by bad weather and hundreds of aftershocks.

After the quake

A powerful earthquake can do a lot of damage if it strikes a city. Buildings fall down and streets get torn apart. People can be hurt by collapsing buildings and some can get trapped under the rubble. Communication and power lines go down, and there is chaos and confusion. Ambulances can have trouble driving through the rubble-strewn streets. Survivors may be left without medical supplies, food or shelter. Sometimes many hours may pass before the outside world wakes up to the disaster and emergency services start arriving.

Danger of disease

Following an earthquake, the local water supply can be contaminated by debris, chemical leaks from damaged factories or the bodies of humans and animals. Disease caused by lack of clean water can be a real danger in the weeks following an earthquake.

I wouldn't drink that if I were you.

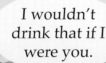

Emergency relief

The first task of emergency workers arriving at the scene of an earthquake is to rescue those trapped under the rubble and give medical treatment to the injured. Once rescued, survivors will need food and shelter. Due to the danger of aftershocks, survivors are usually evacuated as quickly as possible to emergency refugee camps.

If an earthquake strikes...

Your chances of survival are better if you are inside a building. Stand inside a door frame or crouch under a table and place your hands over your head. If you are outside, move away from buildings, trees or power lines that may fall on you.

It's alright, it's just my stomach…

Fascinating fact

Scientists have developed robot cockroaches that can be released into collapsed buildings following an earthquake. They can squeeze through minute, 2.5 mm cracks and crevices to reach survivors.

Yuck!

It's okay, I'm here to help.

In March 1964, Alaska, USA, was rocked by one of the most powerful earthquakes ever recorded. It was so severe it changed the shape of the coastline. The town of Portage sank and had to be abandoned. The port of Valdez was wrecked and had to be rebuilt on safer ground.

Tsunamis occur most often in the Pacific Ocean. This is due to the Ring of Fire – the area around the edge of the Pacific where earthquakes and volcanic eruptions are common.

Quakes and volcanoes

Most tsunamis are caused by undersea earthquakes. When the Earth's crust suddenly slips, a huge volume of water may rush in to fill the gap, or be thrust upwards, setting off a series of massive waves. An underwater volcanic eruption can have a similar effect.

Tsunami wave

Focus

Fault

A tsunami is a series of powerful ocean waves that strike the land, often with devastating consequences. Tsunamis are caused by sudden movements of seawater due to an earthquake, volcanic eruption or landslide. Waves fan outwards in circles from the point of disturbance like ripples from a stone dropped in a pond. As they move across the ocean, tsunami waves aren't very high. But they rear up as they approach the shore. Tsunamis can be very destructive when they hit a coastline, smashing buildings, sweeping away people and animals and flooding the land.

It's a fine day for surfing.

Growing wave

Tsunami waves start off small. A boat sailing over one would scarcely feel it. But they move extremely fast, at up to 965 kph (600 mph). As the wave approaches land, it slows down and rises up. By the time it hits the shore, the wave can be up to 30 metres (98 feet) high – as tall as a 10-storey building.

Seiches

Sometimes strong winds can set off giant waves in enclosed bodies of water, such as lakes. These are called seiches, and they sway back and forth from one side of the lake to the other. As they move up and down a lake, the water level rises and falls at either end, but stays at the same level in the middle.

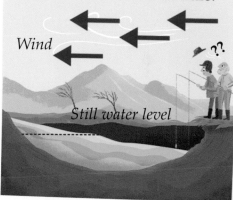

Wind

Still water level

Occasionally, asteroids stray close to the Earth. Most break up in the Earth's atmosphere, but it's possible that a large one may one day strike our planet. If it hits the ocean, it could set off a megatsunami.

Try it yourself

Make your own seiche! Fill a pan halfway with water. With a marker, mark the pan just above the water level halfway along the pan. Push your hand down through the water several times at one end of the pan to set the water moving. Like a seiche, the water level next to the mark will stay the same while it rocks up and down at each end of the pan.

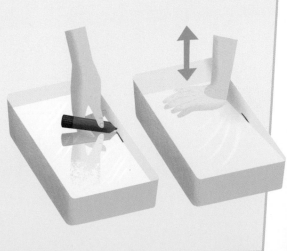

When tsunamis strike

Tsunamis often strike without warning, giving people no time to move to safety. In some cases, the sea first draws back from the land as the approaching tsunami wave drags the sea into itself. This is often accompanied by a hissing, cracking or rumbling sound. As the giant tsunami wave sweeps in, it lifts cars, boats and other objects, and carries them far inland. Many people are injured or killed by being struck by the debris as it's swept along.

A warning from history

Along Japan's coastline, enormous stones have been erected warning people of the danger of tsunamis. Most of these tablets date back to 1896 when two tsunamis killed around 22,000 people. One reads: 'Remember the calamity of the great tsunamis. Do not build any homes below this point.'

Indian Ocean, 2004

On 26 December 2004, a huge earthquake off the coast of Sumatra, Indonesia, set off one of the most devastating tsunamis in history. Entire communities were wiped off the map and up to 283,000 people were killed. Worst affected were Sumatra, Thailand, Sri Lanka and India.

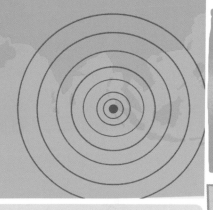

On 27 August 1883, the volcanic island of Krakatau exploded, releasing 25 cubic km (6 cubic miles) of rock and ash. The resulting caldera collapse caused enormous tsunami waves.

Bores

Tsunami waves behave differently depending on the shape of the shore they strike. If a tsunami comes from deep water into a narrow, shallow bay or river, it may appear as a giant breaking wave. This is called a bore, and it can be extremely powerful and destructive.

Here comes a bore.

You mean Andy's arrived?

Can you believe it?

Occasionally, tsunamis produce extremely high waves, especially when they occur in confined spaces. These are called megatsunamis. The biggest recorded occurred at Lituya Bay, Alaska, in 1958, following an earthquake and landslide. The resulting wave destroyed vegetation to a height of 525 metres (1,722 ft)!

We should be safe up here.

Or maybe not!

Emergency rescue

Emergency services must rescue those trapped under rubble, cast adrift in the sea or stuck in trees and on rooftops. The next job is to provide food, shelter and medical treatment to survivors. Finally, the laborious cleanup process begins, as well as the task of rebuilding the community.

After the waves

Tsunamis can cause terrible and long-lasting devastation, especially to fishing communities and tourist destinations on the Pacific coasts, where they occur most often. Many people drown, or are killed by being struck by debris. Survivors often have to cope with injuries, and a lack of food and shelter. Floods can destroy communication and power lines. They can cause sewage to leak into the water supply, leading to outbreaks of diseases such as cholera and typhoid. Roads and harbours are often destroyed, making it hard for emergency services to reach those in need.

Tsunamis also harm marine life. Fish are swept onto the land and left stranded when the water retreats. Debris and leakages from sewage works and factories are washed out to sea, causing pollution.

Identifying the missing

In the chaos following the 2004 Indian Ocean tsunami, many families were separated. People posted photographs of their loved ones online or on the walls of local hospitals. That way some families were reunited, or at least discovered the fate of those they had lost.

Tsunamis and dinosaurs

Around 65 million years ago, a vast 10-km-diameter asteroid struck the sea near Mexico. It would have vaporized a huge volume of water, leaving a giant hole. The sea would have rushed in to fill the hole, creating a megatsunami with waves several kilometres high. The dinosaurs became extinct around this time. Could the two events be connected? Many scientists think so.

The big rock missed us! Yippee!

But what about that big wave?

Fascinating fact

Water is heavier than you might think: a litre weighs 1,000 grams (2.2 lb), so when a large volume of it is moving fast, it becomes very powerful. Even knee-deep water can sweep a person away. A 9-metre (29.5 ft) wave can knock down walls.

Woah!

Tsunamis flatten forests, flood farmland and erode soil. They hurl salty seawater over the land, killing vegetation. Human activities have damaged coral reefs and mangrove forests that would otherwise have protected the land from tsunamis.

25

Volcano proofing

Some communities have tried to defend themselves from the outflows of volcanic eruptions. In Japan and Indonesia, they have built 'sabo dams', special defences that block debris carried by lahars while allowing the muddy water through. In some places barriers have been erected to divert lava flows away from towns.

In Japan, traditional houses made of wood and bamboo collapse easily in earthquakes, but are less likely to cause injury than bricks. They do burn easily though, and many Japanese earthquakes have been followed by disastrous fires.

Rebuilding

After a natural disaster, communities must be rebuilt. The first stage of rebuilding involves clearing debris and demolishing any unsafe buildings. Most people do not wish to move to safer locations, so communities are usually rebuilt in the same place. People also tend to want their rebuilt town to look the same as, or similar to, the destroyed one. This desire to conserve traditions must be balanced against the importance of rebuilding using techniques that will make the new town better able to withstand future disasters.

Quake proofing

Buildings in earthquake-prone areas are constructed with flexible frameworks that allow for some movement. Some structures have a central, firmly rooted column, and walls that can move when the ground shifts. Other buildings 'float' on systems of springs and padded cylinders that act like shock absorbers.

Timber is a good building material in earthquake-prone areas, because it's light and flexible. However, it's a bad material in tsunami-prone areas because it floats and can become a deadly weapon if carried away by the wave.

Tsunami proofing

Few buildings can withstand the enormous force of a tsunami wave. However, they have a better chance if built on stilts, so the water can flow beneath them. It also helps if the building is constructed diagonally to the wave front. If the wave hits the corner first, the pressure on the building is greatly reduced.

Maybe it's time we popped round to see the neighbours!

Can you believe it?

On 23 January 1973, the ground split open in a town on the island of Heimaey near Iceland. Lava, ash and steam erupted from it, and the crack soon became a fissure 1.6 kilometres (1 mile) long.

Predicting disasters

Scientists are getting better at predicting disasters. They can monitor volcanoes and the fault lines between tectonic plates for signs that could indicate a coming eruption, quake or tsunami.

For example, vulcanologists (volcano experts) take gas samples from a volcano's vent. If the gas contains sulphur dioxide, then magma is probably rising and an eruption may be imminent. They also use seismographs to detect earth tremors. Vulcanologists used these techniques to predict the 1991 eruption of Mount Pinatubo. As a result, tens of thousands of lives were saved.

I think this one may be about to blow…

Looking out for earthquakes

Seismologists set up networks of monitoring stations in quake-prone regions. They use sensitive instruments to check for tiny shifts in rocks, or seismographs to detect foreshocks that may herald a major earthquake. Cracking or bulging rocks, or gas or water leaking from the ground near a fault are also signs that a quake may be imminent.

What does it say?

I can't read it. There's too much shaking.

Tsunami Warnings

Pressure sensors on the seabed can detect tsunami waves out in the ocean. As the wave passes overhead, the weight on the sensors increases, and a message is sent via sonar to a surface buoy, then relayed to a satellite. Scientists use this data to predict when and where a tsunami will strike, and send out warnings to the countries affected.

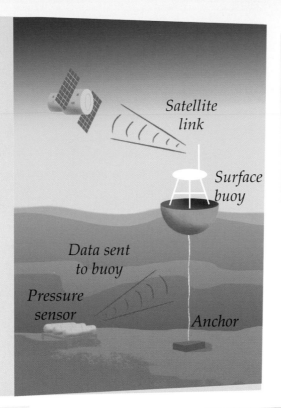

Satellite link

Surface buoy

Data sent to buoy

Pressure sensor

Anchor

By studying the intervals between earthquakes in the past and measuring the movement of plates, seismologists can calculate when an area is due for a large earthquake. Unfortunately, they can't say exactly when it will happen.

Being prepared

People living in disaster-prone areas must always be prepared – when warnings come they will often have very little time to save themselves. If a tsunami is coming, go into a sturdy building and climb to the highest floor. If caught by a wave, grab a floating object and let the water carry you.

Inflatables

The next megatsunami?

When the Cumbre Vieja volcano in the Canary Islands next erupts, it could cause a huge landslide of rock into the sea. Some scientists believe this could set off a megatsunami that could devastate the eastern United States, including cities like New York and Boston.

Glossary

Aftershock Tremors that occur as the ground settles down after an earthquake.

Asteroid A large rock hurtling through space, usually hundreds to thousands of metres across.

Avalanche A mass of snow, ice and rocks falling rapidly down a mountainside.

Body wave Seismic waves that travel through the Earth, as opposed to surface waves that travel across the surface.

Caldera A giant hole formed when the ground collapses into the empty magma chamber of a volcano.

Convergent fault A boundary between tectonic plates where the plates come together (converge).

Crust The rocky, outermost layer of a planet such as Earth.

Divergent fault A boundary between tectonic plates where the plates separate and new land is formed from lava welling up.

Epicentre The place on the surface of the Earth above the point where an earthquake originates.

Erode Wear (something) away by wind, water or other natural forces.

Evacuate Remove (someone) from a place of danger to a safer place.

Fault A boundary between two or more tectonic plates.

Fissure A long, narrow opening made by cracking or splitting.

Focus The point underground where an earthquake originates.

Foreshock The shaking of the ground that comes before an earthquake.

Hot spot A place in the middle of a tectonic plate where magma forces its way to the surface.

Igneous rock Rock formed from the solidification of lava or magma.

Lahar A destructive mudflow on the slopes of a volcano.

Lava Molten or solid rock on the surface of the Earth that has come from a volcano.

Magma Hot, semi-liquid material beneath the Earth's crust.

Magma chamber A magma-filled space deep under a volcano.

Mantle The hot region of the Earth's interior between the crust and the core.

Megatsunami A huge wave caused by something very big, such as an asteroid or landslide, suddenly falling into water.

Pyroclastic flow A thick cloud of red-hot ash and rock that flows down the side of a volcano.

Refugee Someone forced to leave their home in order to escape war, persecution or natural disaster.

Seamount An undersea volcano that forms an island.

Seismograph An instrument that measures and records earthquakes.

Seismologist An expert on earthquakes.

Shield volcano A low, wide volcano made of lava flows piled on top of one another.

Stratovolcano A cone-shaped volcano made of alternate layers of lava and ash.

Subduction zone An area where one tectonic plate is pushed beneath another.

Tectonic plates The giant plates that together make up the Earth's crust.

Transform fault A boundary between tectonic plates where the plates slide against each other.

Tsunami A series of massive waves caused by undersea disturbances.

Vent A hole through the middle of a volcano from which ash and lava escape.

Vulcanologist An expert on volcanoes.

Index